Meditative Mandalas
Relaxation through color

Elaine Catherine Lombardo

For my family and closest friends,
who's love and support
has always been the light in my darkness.

Thank you for believing in me
and helping me to remember
to believe in myself.

Meditative Mandalas
Relaxation through color
Elaine Catherine Lombardo

Explore your creativity, expand your mind, and release tension and anxiety through color! By focusing your mind on the intricate patters and repetitive coloring, you will find yourself increasingly slipping into a calmer and more tranquil state of mind and spirit. With time and practice, you will find that these Mandalas and the use of color will allow you to practice a form of controlled meditation, and even just a few minutes a day will assist you in letting go of your stress. The designs I created range from the basic to the complex, allowing people of all ages and artistic levels to explore this relaxing activity.

Some benefits of coloring are:

Relaxation

Meditation

Therapeutic

Stress relief

Perfect for all ages

Stimulates creativity

Helps focus the mind

Basic to complex designs for all levels

Great for coloring or filling in zentangle patterns

A mix of spiritual, mental and whimsical designs

Used by educators, parents and care-takers as color therapy for children and adults with special needs

25 unique mandalas in both single and full page patterns

"The Lotus"

"Focus"

"Mother"

"Fleur-de-Lis"

"Jewel"

"The Five Elements"

"Rain"

"Sorrow"

"Divinity"

"The Infinite"

"Inner Eye"

"The Masculine"

"Eternal"

"Emptiness"

"Terra"

"How Many Owls?"

"Spiral"

"Family Devotion"

"Adoration"

"Passion"

"The Feminine"

"Guardian"

"Creation"

"Rebirth"

"How Many Cats?"

Thank you for purchasing my book.
I hope you find it relaxing, soothing and comforting.
Allow yourself to get lost in the pattern
and don't be afraid to use lots of color.
Free your mind and you will find
peace.